Henry Adams Thompson

Demand for an educated ministry

an address delivered before the students and trustees of Western College

Henry Adams Thompson

Demand for an educated ministry
an address delivered before the students and trustees of Western College

ISBN/EAN: 9783337377441

Printed in Europe, USA, Canada, Australia, Japan

Cover: Foto ©Paul-Georg Meister /pixelio.de

More available books at **www.hansebooks.com**

DEMAND FOR AN EDUCATED MINISTRY.

AN ADDRESS,

DELIVERED BEFORE THE

Students and Trustees of Western College,

WESTERN, IOWA,

AT THE

ANNUAL COMMENCEMENT,

BY

REV. H. A. THOMPSON, A. M.,

PROFESSOR OF MATHEMATICS IN OTTERBEIN UNIVERSITY,

WESTERVILLE, OHIO.

DAYTON, OHIO:
UNITED BRETHREN PRINTING ESTABLISHMENT.
1865.

ADDRESS.

Young Gentlemen:

I speak to-night to those of you who trust, that in the providence of God, you have been called to preach the Gospel of Christ to a ruined world. A fearful responsibility is upon him who attempts to teach the young, because in his hands rests their present and eternal destiny. A still greater responsibility rests upon him who is instrumental in forming and molding the character of the embassador for Christ. In benefitting him, he indirectly blesses hundreds of others. In leading him astray, he ruins for time and eternity. Trusting in the God of our spirits to teach you aright wherein I shall fail, I shall present to you some considerations showing the urgent demand, at the present time, for an Educated Ministry. This subject should have the careful consideration of all intelligent, Christian men, because in proper conclusions upon it rest your own welfare and the success and prosperity of the Church.

In approaching this subject, I am immediately met by an oft-repeated objection which it might be well enough to dispose of in the beginning. "Are not the Apostles said to have been *ignorant and unlearned men*, and were they not successful?" If we should confess this, for argument sake, and infer that we, therefore, need the same class of men now, we would show greater presumption than common sense or piety. Acknowledging them to have perfectly suited the age in which they lived, it does not at all follow that they would suit this age. The world has not been stationary. In every department there has been progress. The position of affairs has materially changed. New impulses have been at work. New currents of thought have been formed. In short, a new age is upon us, and we want men, in every respect suited to this age.

They were "*unlearned and common people*," the original tells us. None of them, perhaps, except Paul, had ever sat at the feet of Gamaliel. They were not men who were accustomed to administer the affairs of government, or to take part in civil transactions, but they came from the common walks of life. Were they ignorant men? Some of them have written books. Do not them books completely refute this assertion? It requires no skillful eye to see that they were men of sterling good sense, prudent and intelligent. John's writings show him to have been well acquainted with the schools of Grecian Philosophy, and the knowledge he there obtained he made subservient to Christian purposes. Luke was a physician. The remainder, by their writings and their actions, give unmistakable evidence that they were men who understood their great work and were fitted for it.

Who calls them ignorant? Read the record. The rulers and elders and scribes, with Ananias and Caiaphas, were assembled together, and, having listened to the addresses of these men, they perceived that they were unlettered. So they may have been. Ignorant, as regards a knowledge of the traditions of the Sadducees, and Pharisees, in which consisted their greatest amount of learning, but skilled in that knowledge necessary to instruct and enlighten the heart.

These men were instructed for *three* long years by that best of all teachers, Him, " who spake as never man spake." He found them dull students, and had occasion to reprove them for their tardiness in learning the great truths which he came to teach. Almost wearied in his efforts he says to one, "Have

I been so long time with you, and yet hast thou not known me, Philip?" He resorted to the most simple illustrations, to the affairs of every day life with which they were supposed to be familiar, in order the more thoroughly and effectually to imbue their minds with a knowledge of the doctrines he came to preach. After having labored faithfully to instruct them in the things pertaining to Christianity, for fear they may not fully understand his meaning, or may have some misconceptions of the truth, he presses home upon their attention the appropriate and pertinent question, "Have ye understood all these things?" After he had given them line upon line, and precept upon precept, for the space of three years, even then they were not fitted for the great work. They must "tarry at Jerusalem until indued with power from on high." They may interpose objections and be anxious to enter the field, but the command was to wait, and wait they did.

"But," says one, "they were inspired." So their writings testify. We have no account that they were inspired in their ordinary administrations. Their powers may have been strengthened and invigorated, yet we have no other evidence than that they were left to the ordinary and natural use of their powers. If they were inspired and needed not to acquire knowledge in the ordinary ways, does it therefore follow that because we are not inspired, we should remain ignorant? So much the stronger reason why we should use all the means at our command, so as to bring ourselves nearer the position occupied by the apostles.

Look at the *effects* of apostolic preaching. Good resulted. Many were converted; churches were established; the people of God were strengthened. Wherever they went the power of the Most High accompanied them, and that power was manifested in the elevation of mankind. If ignorant men can go forth now and accomplish the same great work; can thus instruct and edify the church; can establish and build up Christian associations; can lay the foundation for good results to come; can thus benefit their fellow men and promote the good of their Master's cause; if, in the midst of the evils surrounding them, they can show themselves "wise as serpents and harmless as doves," then let us as a church send forth none but ignorant men. As long as they can not do this, and as long as their influence is weakened and their people perish for lack of knowledge, let us not adduce the example of the apostles in support of the proposition that God demands ignorant men to stand upon the walls of Zion.

That Christ would appoint ignorant men to be his standard-bearers, is utterly irreconcilable with the whole tenor of Scripture and the whole course of his own life. That he did do so, is contrary to all Jewish history. Perhaps there never was a people so universally educated as the Jews. Many of our Savior's remarks indicate this. How often he asked them "Have ye not read what Moses saith?" "Have ye not read in the Scriptures?" evidently implying that the common people (because he addressed them) could and did read the writings of Moses and the prophets. We are told that when Pilate placed over the head of the Redeemer at his crucifixion the inscription in "letters of Greek and Latin and Hebrew," that "this title was read by many of the Jews." It was enjoined upon the people to teach their children to read and understand the ordinances which God had made known. "The words which I command thee this day shall be in thy heart, and thou shalt teach them diligently to thy children, and thou shalt write them upon the posts of thine house and upon thy gates."

Under the Jewish dispensation, the Priests and Levites were not illiterate men. The Levitical cities were places of learning. The clergy, judges, lawyers, physicians and teachers of the people came principally from the tribe of Levi. By the law of Moses, this tribe had no inheritance in the division of the land. It was chosen out for the service of the sanctuary, and had to be supported by contributions from the whole nation. From this tribe came the priests, who had charge of the tabernacle and the temple. They scattered themselves in different parts of the country, instructing their countrymen. They were employed in writing and circulating the Scriptures, and in explaining them to the people whenever they had an opportunity. They were to study the law diligently, and be ready to answer inquiries, which were made by others, pertaining to religion.

Scribes had a similar business; they were, originally, men ready with the pen, but the name came to denote simply a learned man. And as learning among the Jews was confined principally to the sacred book, the word came to denote one who was skilled in the law of God; one whose business it was to procure copies of the Scriptures and explain their meaning. Ezra is called "a ready scribe of the law of Moses." They were sometimes called *doctors* of the law and *lawyers*, because they interpreted the law. They were consulted in all cases of doubt or uncertainty about the truth of the Scriptures.

Such were the men appointed by God under the old Jewish dispensation, to instruct the people in divine truth. Not ignorant and untutored men, but scholars—the most learned men of the nation. The people were intelligent, and needed intelligent teachers. A whole tribe was set apart for the purpose of educating and training themselves for their appointed work. Did any doubt rest upon the mind of any one, these men were called in to interpret. They explained and enforced the Scriptures in public and private. "No illiterate man or mechanic was allowed to speak in the synagogue under any circumstances, but only the learned."—(*Jennings'*

Jew. Ant. B. II., C. 2.) I can find no instance in Old Testament history where God commanded ignorant and illiterate men to stand before the people, and statedly declare his law unto them. In all cases men thoroughly qualified were chosen, or if not thus fitted, they underwent the necessary training before they were sent forth upon their mission. Has God changed his policy now?

More than this, the Jews had *special* schools for the education of their ministers. Says the learned Dr. Lightfoot: " It has been the way of God to instruct his people by a studious and learned ministry ever since he gave a written word to instruct them. Who were the standing ministry of Israel all the time from the giving of the law till the captivity in Babylon? Not prophets or inspired men. These were but occasional teachers. They were the priests and Levites, who became learned in the law by study. And for this end they were distributed into *forty-eight* cities, as so many universities, where they studied law *together*, and from these were sent out into the several synagogues to teach the people. " The same author also says that " contributions were made for the support of these students while they studied in the universities, as well as afterward when they preached in the synagogues. " Further on he says: " There were among the Jews authorized individual teachers of great eminence, who had divinity schools in which they expounded the law to their scholars or disciples. Of these divinity schools, there is frequent mention made among the Jewish writers, more especially of the schools of *Hillel* and *Shammai*." Such a divinity professor was Gamaliel, at whose feet the great apostle of the gentiles received his education.

Very early in Jewish history we read of the schools of the prophets. In one of them Samuel himself taught theology. The most prominent of these schools were at *Naioth*, *Bethel*, *Gilgal* and *Jericho*. A large number of students were in

attendance upon these institutions. They were educated in the knowledge of religion, and were under the supervision of some prophet, who was generally inspired. They were thus qualified to become public preachers, which was a part of the business of prophets on Sabbath days and festivals. The prophets whom God inspired, were generally chosen from these schools.

In the formation and establishment of the church, God took care that the messengers who declared his will to the people, should on all occasions be fully competent for the task. They underwent the necessary training until they were workmen that needed not to be ashamed. These schools received the Lord's approbation. He himself grew in wisdom and stature, as did all the prophets. He came from the lower class of people, but was not content to remain upon the same level with them. At the early age of twelve, he astonished his hearers by his knowledge; and when he commenced his public work, all the treasures of knowledge abounded in his intellectual nature.

I proceed to notice the direct arguments in favor of an Educated Ministry.

The very fact that the Scriptures have been written in what are now called the dead languages, seems to demand this. The very Spirit that gave the apostles utterance upon the day of Pentecost, so that Romans, Jews, Parthians, Medes and Cretans, and all that were assembled, could hear and understand them in their own language, could as easily have given them the inspiration to multiply written translations of the Bible, as do what he did. He did not do this. He has given us the glowing imagery of the Old Testament couched in the Hebrew language, and the pointed logic of the New, in the Greek. It is true we have excellent translations of these, but they are only translations. It is the Hebrew and Greek words that are inspired, and not our translations. The words are the very words of God, in which thoughts, like precious gems of metal, are locked, requiring only the key of study to open them. He who can not read these, has never seen the inspired word of God as it really is; as it came from God himself. He has not heard the oracle of the temple speak, but merely some fallible man like himself, standing at the door repeating as well as he could, the utterance. He has not seen the original portrait of God's will, as drawn by himself, as every teacher should. He has merely looked upon a second-hand picture—a human copy of the portrait. The very fact that God has designedly locked up his richest truths in these dead languages, strongly indicates that he would have the guides of his people study to "show themselves approved," and that he is not one who patronizes stupidity, or encourages willful ignorance.

This leads to another thought: *No man can properly understand the word of God unless he is to some extent conversant with these languages.* Every student knows that the best translations at our command can not, do not give the true meaning of the original. There are nice shades of meaning, minute distinctions, that will throw light upon the whole thought, and which a translation can not give. In the formation of the original word, its derivations and modifications, its history—because a nation's history is written in its language—there is often embodied a world of meaning, vast magazines of thought, which only the words themselves can reveal. The skillful linguist sees all these things, and they modify and correct all his impressions of truth. They suggest to him new thoughts in the enunciation of that truth. We have an excellent translation, and yet often the precise meaning is not given; at least not given so as to be free from ambiguity. In the Hebrew especially, the emotional element is necessary to a correct understanding, and yet it is almost impossible to render this, and frequently in our version it has not been attempted. The emotion very often rests in some little particle, some particular collocation of the words, and very often in the absence of the words themselves. The very moment we attempt to put it into words, and make a distinct logical statement, we lose all its power. We may use periphrastic forms (even this we can not do unless linguists), resort to various expedients, so as to approximate the meaning, but even then we have lost the intensity. We may dissect the body, see where the life was; but, to a great extent, the life itself, the all-animating power, is gone. Our translation often fails to give us as much of that life as it might do. In the present translation we read: "From everlasting unto everlasting thou art God;" a simple statement. In the original we read: "From everlasting unto everlasting thou—oh, God!" a sentence containing the same thought as the other, and yet more effectually brought home to us through the medium of the heavenly emotion accompanying it. "Thy throne, oh, God! is forever and ever." Throw out the interpolations, and you read: "Thy throne—oh God!—forever and ever." If the reader can put himself in the position of the writer, he finds in the meaning of a particle, or the omission of a word sometimes, an intensity of emotion which the reader of the mere translation can never get. "The fool hath said in his heart, there is no God." Now read: "The fool says in his heart—no God." How slight the change, and yet how great the difference! In one case a simple statement; in the other, the poor fool talking to himself, or musing, as the original strictly teaches, or rather the foolish thoughts talking with each other. "God is not in all his thoughts," says the common version, implying that he is in some. Says the Hebrew, "No God—all his thoughts." It is not a forgetfulness. The conceptions, ideas, thoughts, and emotions, indeed his whole soul is Godless, wholly atheistic.

In the omission of words, sometimes we see this richness, this depth of meaning. Says our translation, "Let it alone this year, and if it bear fruit, well;" now read the original, "Let it alone this year, and if it bear fruit"—no answer given, and yet more expressive than words could make it. "Take no thought for your life, what ye shall eat," says our version. The Greek reads, "Do not be troubled or annoyed about your life," implying not that we should care nothing about the affairs of this life, but that they should not be allowed to trouble us. He who confers all other blessings, will also grant these. "And John was baptizing at Enon, near to Salem, because there was much water there," says our version. Therefore, argue our Baptist brethren, if he needed much water, he must have desired to immerse the people. Says the original, "Many streams" (*pollu udata*), many little streams or creeks, for which that country was remarkable, and not one deep river. "But to sit on my right hand or on my left hand is not mine to give, but it shall be given to to them for whom it is prepared." Our translation would imply that it did not rest in the hands of the Savior, but that some other had the disposing of it. This is not the true rendering. Says the Greek, "To sit," &c., "is not mine to give, except to those for whom it is prepared." If these persons are those to whom I have appointed this position, then they shall have it.

These few selections out of a thousand are sufficient to convince you that the minister who has access to the original Scriptures holds in his hands a power which the reader of the mere translation can never possess. He has access to a vast treasury, which no one save the scholar can behold.

Much other knowledge is necessary to a proper understanding of the Scriptures. Every age has its distinguishing characteristics. The peculiar modes of thought, and all the surrounding circumstances which give power to ideas in one age of the world, in another have lost their force. We must place ourselves in the condition of the people, and see from their stand-point, if we would understand as they did. We must become familiar with oriental expressions and peculiarities of thought, with eastern imagery, the structure of Hebrew poetry, the manners and customs of the inhabitants, their inner and public life, their various kinds of business, the workings of their social, religious and political systems, the great central truths which every-where stirred the nation, the peculiarities of the country, its geography and the nature of its scenery, with its influence upon the training of the people and the production of their literature, the wealth and grandeur of its cities, its power for defensive and aggressive war, the influence of other nations in controlling its life progress, a knowledge of the history of other peoples with its bearing upon the fulfillment of prophecy, the great part they respectively acted in carrying out the designs of Deity; where the particular books of Scripture were written, when and by whom, the nature of the authors, age in which they lived, a knowledge of the arts and sciences which the people then possessed, a general history of the literature of the day, the aim of the writers, the class of persons for whom they wrote, and the schools of philosophy then prevalent; how these books have been preserved, and whether or not we have the inspired Scriptures; have there been any interpolations, or is the copy correct? are the statements therein recorded mere theories, or facts capable of being substantiated by testimony? a knowledge of the facts of history in their bearing upon the interpretation of Scripture scenes; the records of Egypt, and the stony pillars of Assyria and Babylon; the teachings of geology, as confirming the Mosaic account of creation; the facts of physiological science, as asserting the unity of man; of chemistry, as illustrating many passages of sacred Scripture.

I need not enumerate. Not a fact in nature, not a page in history, not a truth in mental and moral science, not a principle in philosophy, scarcely a thought in all the vast range of literature, art, or science, but may be made subservient to the great work of unfolding the meaning of divine truth.

I argue the need of a thorough education, *in order to make the minister a skillful teacher;* "a workman that needeth not to be ashamed." To this end every science may pay tribute, and every field of thought afford material. His commission commands him to "go teach all nations." It is not enough that men have been converted; they must be edified and instructed; must be trained and nurtured in religion. It is not enough that an army be raised; it must be disciplined and led forth to battle. It is not enough that the farmer sows his seed; he must cultivate and train and prune until he can gather the full sheaf into his barn. To instruct, was the business of Christ himself. The minister must come in contact with all classes of mind; men of various shades of opinion; men of varied intellectual culture and diversity of talent. He must be prepared to meet the ignorant and the intelligent; to solve the doubts of one, and put to silence the sophisms of the other. He must be all things to all men. He must be a man of varied knowledge, of ripe thought, of logical reasoning powers, and skillful in the doctrines and interpretations of Scripture.

A fine example, showing to the minister the necessity for having boundless resources of knowledge, is found in the ministerial life of the Savior. His aim was to instruct the people, and every thought, every illustration from nature, every fact of science, every truth in history that would avail in the accomplishment of his purpose, was employed. What beautiful simplicity and adaptability in all his teachings! How pertinent his thoughts, and how opportunely selected!

In his hands, the fowls of the air, the beasts of the field, the lily of the valley, the sand of the sea-shore, the hair of the head, the thirst of the widow, the unfruitful fig-tree, the cities of the hill, all become instructive and impressive sermons. Standing by Jacob's well, he represents true piety under the image of "living water." When he meets the fishermen, he asks, "What man is there of you, whom if his son ask a fish, will he give him a serpent?" After multiplying the loaves, having the minds of his hearers intent upon the miracle, he tells them, "I am the bread of life; he that cometh unto me shall never hunger." When seed-time approaches, he exclaims, "Say ye not four months, and then cometh the harvest?" While teaching his disciples, and observing a city upon an adjoining hill, he tells them, "Ye are a city set upon a hill that can not be hid." While the sheep are standing around the temple, ready to be sacrificed for the feast of the Passover, he says, "I am the good shepherd, and lay down my life for the sheep." Having partaken of the wine, and made it a symbol of his blood, he tells them, "I am the vine, ye are the branches."

When on his way from Capernaum to the lake, treading among lilies, and with sparrows above his head, he teaches his disciples of a Providence who cares for them. At the feast of the tabernacles, while the people were drawing water out of the fountain of Siloam to pour upon the sacrifices, and while they sing, "With joy shall ye draw water out of the well of salvation," Jesus tells them, "If any man thirst, let him come to me and drink." Immediately before giving sight to the blind, he proclaims, "I am the light of the world." In seed-time he relates the parable of the man "who went forth to sow." In the spring, when the branches put forth their leaves, he says, "Behold the fig-tree and all the trees; when they now shoot forth, ye say and know of yourselves that summer is nigh at hand; so likewise ye, when ye see these things come to pass, know that the kingdom of God is nigh at hand."

In his parables you see the same wisdom, the same happy simplicity. In this method of instruction, practiced by all nations, he excelled. You see him using the most simple circumstances in life to press home upon his hearers the thrilling truths of the gospel. By the ten virgins, he teaches us the necessity of a preparation for heaven; the pearl of great price, the exceeding value of Christ as offered to us in the gospel; the talents, the improvement of our time and all our powers for our Master's use; the house and kingdom divided against themselves, the necessity of union; the seed growing secretly, the silent yet efficient influence of divine truth; the blind leading the blind, the great danger of trusting to false teachers; the good Samaritan, the necessity of showing mercy toward our neighbor; the lost sheep, the love of God in caring for sinful man.

All these subjects are happily chosen. The plan is wisely unfolded. The narration is interesting, and the meaning definite and clear. No story too simple, no allusion too magnificent, no thought too grand, if it will but illustrate the truth, and rivet it more firmly upon the minds of the hearers.

We have another example in Scripture, showing us how all knowledge may be made useful in the exposition of truth; the example of a man we would do well to imitate.

Ephesus was a prominent city of the East, renowned for its learning and its idolatry. Here stood the wonder of the world, the pride of Ionic wealth and Ionic architecture—the temple of the great Ephesian Diana. Here flourished magic, with all the tricks of Eastern jugglery. Thousands of traders in talismans here lived and grew wealthy on the superstitions of the foolish people. Here were . celebrated schools of rhetoric, learning, and philosophy, that the Greeks were always accustomed to support wherever their language was spoken ; schools which, if they did not aid materially in the discovery of much new truth, at least promoted a certain kind of intellectual culture. Here, too, the Jew, that homeless one, who had a foothold but no resting-place upon almost every soil, had built a synagogue. Here were Jews, the disciples of John the Baptist, waiting patiently for that great Deliverer whom he foretold to be near at hand.

Paul enters Ephesus. He had been here previous to this time, but the visit was a transient one. He goes into the synagogue, and preaches to his countrymen. Although a servant of God and apostle to the gentiles, he has not renounced his nationality. The gospel which he preaches is but a consummation of that which Moses and the prophets taught. How full of rich suggestions ; what food for thought in his conversations and discourses in the synagogue for the space of three months, while one after another of those who had long been agitated by conflicting theories, and who had long been wavering, now yield to his arguments, and with joy acknowledge Christ to be the Savior of the world— the Messiah that was to come. Parties are formed. A controversy arises among them. A few adhere to the apostle, and these form the germ of a religious community. But Paul was more catholic in his views ; more noble-hearted, more liberal, perhaps, than any Jew that ever preceded him. He looks beyond his own precincts and interest to offer the gospel to Grecian Asia. He wants to attack paganism in its very stronghold. Here where Idolatry has raised her temples, and laid the foundations deep, he will ply the most powerful engines of his artillery. Here at the very confluence of Egyptian, Grecian, Roman, and Oriental idolatries, he will propagate truth that will overturn this great temple, drive the idols to the moles and bats, and send the gospel of the Redeemer throughout the land. He is not content until he

can stand where he shall have power, with the great lever of
of the gospel, to move the world of superstition and degrada-
tion that surrounds him.

That little band of disciples, as they came together for
worship and fraternal communion, could give him no such a
position. He burns with a holy ambition to dare and do for
his Master. This desired position he found, through the kind
providence of God, in one of the schools of Grecian Philosophy with which that city could not fail to be supplied. In
these schools there was a professed inquiry after truth, and
accordingly a freedom of debate and discussion was allowed,
which gave abundant advantages. A man of letters, skilled
in the wisdom of the Greeks and the knowledge of the
Scriptures, he availed himself of the kindness of one of these
teachers. He participated in these discussions. Says the
historian Luke, he was "found disputing daily in the school
of one Tyrannus; and this he continued for the space of two
years." Here was the offer, and he accepted. No better
opportunity for preaching to the gentile population, in fact
the entire population of city and country, could have been
found, than the one which now presented itself. He flung
himself into the midst of the struggle, and with a brawny
arm at his command, dealt mighty blows for his Master's
cause. A learned man; gifted with all the acquisitions of
the schools, and a knowledge of the arts and sciences; with
unsurpassed eloquence and logic at his command; every
literary and scientific argument must be brought into service,
to do battle for the truth. Day after day he debated in that
literary institution for the space of two years; and so successful was he in diffusing light among the inhabitants of that
city, as well as of the surrounding country, that Luke tells us,
"All they who dwelt in Asia heard the word of the Lord
Jesus, both Jew and Greek." The light which he was daily
putting forth in the school of Tyrannus had its effect upon

other minds, men of high intellect, and was borne by them into other parts of the country. Darkness was being scattered as by a visitation from on high. Not only was the effect seen upon those who directly felt its power, but it was noticed in the great change of public sentiment. The established idolatry was beginning to lose its hold upon the minds of the people, so that the branches of trade which depended upon their support, were materially affected. A glorious tribute is paid to the labors of this apostle by the craftsmen, who complained that "not alone in Ephesus, but almost throughout all Asia, this Paul hath persuaded and turned away much people, saying that there be no gods which are made with hands."—Acts. xix., 26.

After such a noble record, made by the sacred penman, of the great value of learning in upholding and diffusing the truth, let no man attempt to denounce these twin sisters, Religion and Learning; above all things, let that man never be a minister of the everlasting gospel.

There are texts which no minister can explain and enforce without at least a partial knowledge of the sciences. How can he rightly divide the word of truth and edify his hearers and receive the approbation of his God in discussing such texts as the following: "Who maketh Arcturus, Orion, and Pleiades, and the chambers of the South;" "Seek Him that maketh the Seven Stars and Orion?" How can he adequately appreciate the Psalmist's teaching, "The heavens declare the glory of God, and the firmament showeth his handiwork," if he be ignorant of the the first principles of astronomical science? When he has been instructed in Botany, he can properly "consider the lilies of the field." Having learned Geology, then can he better enforce the truth, that "in the beginning God created the heavens and the earth," and utterly silence the cavils of infidelity, that would deprive us of a God, and make our world "a mighty maze and all without a plan." With a knowledge of the first principles of Physiology, and the history of medical science, he can make even infidels bear testimony to the truth that "God hath of one blood made all the nations of men to dwell upon the face of the earth." How often have the words, "If thine enemy hunger, feed him; if he thirst, give him drink; for in so doing thou shalt heap coals of fire on his head," been quoted to show how refined a feeling of revenge may be obtained by returning good for evil! How forcible the reference when Chemistry tells us that that this is "a beautiful metaphor taken from the observance of the ancient practice of smelting ores with carbonaceous fuel, and meaning to subdue an enemy by kindness as metals are melted and reduced by fire." With a knowledge of the principles and laws governing the evaporation of fluids, how scientifically correct the text, "All the rivers run into the sea, yet the sea is not full; unto the place from whence the rivers come, thither do they return again." If he has examined the science of Meteorology, and made himself familiar with the laws by which the system of winds is governed, as far as they have been discovered by our ablest philosophers, how much better fitted to explain the text, "The wind goeth toward the south, and turneth about unto the north; it whirleth about continually, and the wind returneth again according to his circuits."

When he speaks of the overthrow of Sodom and Gomorrah he has the testimony of an officer of our own navy (Lieutenant Lynch), who labored faithfully, and succeeded in demonstrating the truthfulness of the Scripture statement concerning the destruction of these cities. Layard has disentombed from Nineveh the strongest corroborations of its past history, and has found upon the sculptured marble, testimony confirming the account of the miracle said in the Scriptures to have been performed in the case of the prophet Jonah.

If he would learn the lessons, he could learn and communicate the knowledge that is embodied in the prophecies of Scripture and their fulfillment; if he would open up the vast treasures of information contained therein, and instruct the people so that they may be ready to give an answer for the faith that is in them, how extensive and how varied should be his acquirements. What lessons of God's care and protection, as well as withering effects of his wrath, may be learned in the past and present history of the Jewish nation, of Babylon, Philistia, Moab, Damascus, Media, Egypt, Assyria, Idumea, Arabia, Tyre, Edom, and the lives of Cyrus and Sennacherib, with the thousand other cases of prophecy mentioned in holy writ? Every thing bearing upon the fulfillment of these prophecies needs to be examined. The records of history must be searched, and the accounts of intelligent travelers who have visited these renowned lands of the East, and who have been compelled, often unwillingly, to bear testimony to the truth of Scripture history, must be studied. Productions throwing light upon the present condition of nations; the revelations of a Rawlinson or a Layard; the discoveries of our most indefatigable pioneers; the records of monuments illustrating Scripture scenes and substantiating Scripture assertions,—all form a part of the minister's furniture, if he would show himself a workman of God.

An interesting example, showing the great value of a knowledge of sacred and profane history in understanding many passages of revelation, and thus indirectly confirming the truth of holy writ, is found in the thirty-ninth chapter and first verse of Isaiah. "At that time Merodach-baladan, the son of Baladan, king of Babylon, sent letters and a present to Hezekiah," &c. In regard to this statement of the prophet, no little difficulty has been felt by commentators, and it is only lately that the difficulty has been removed, and in such a way as to furnish a striking demonstration of the minute accuracy of the sacred narrative.

The difficulty arose, first, because this king of Babylon is nowhere else mentioned in sacred history; second, the kingdom of Assyria was yet flourishing, and Babylon was one of its dependencies.—(2d Kings xvii., 24; 2d Chron. xxxiii., 11). These examples prove that at the time of Hezekiah, Babylon was dependent on the Assyrian king. Who, then, was this Merodach-baladan, king of Babylon? If he was simply governor of the city, how could he send an embassy to the Jewish sovereign, then at war with his lord? Until lately, Scripture interpreters could give no satisfactory reply.

"In this darkness of doubt," says Dr. Wiseman, "we must have continued, and the apparent contradiction of this text to other passages would have remained inexplicable, had not the progress of modern oriental study brought to light a document of most remarkable antiquity. This is nothing less than a fragment of Berosus, preserved in the chronicle of Eusebius. This interesting fragment informs us that after Sennacherib's brother had governed Babylon, as Assyrian viceroy, Acises unjustly possessed himself of the supreme command. After thirty days he was murdered by Merodach-baladan, who usurped the sovereignty for six months, when he was in turn killed, and was succeeded by Elibus. But after three years, Sennacherib collected an army, gave the usurper battle, conquered and took him prisoner. Having once more reduced Babylon to his obedience, he left his son Assordan, the Esorhaddan of Scripture, as governor of the city."—(*Sci. & Rev. p.* 369.)

No man can have a proper conception of himself, of God, or of the great theme of redemption, and of course can not teach others, unless he be a man of knowledge. The ignorant man looks upon the heavens above him with "a brute unconscious gaze," not thinking of any aim in their creation, save his own pleasure and gratification. The man of science, with the aid of the telescope, converts those twinkling orbs "that shine like diadems on the brow of night," into so many vast and majestic spheres, infinitely superior to our little globe, perhaps peopled by millions of intelligent beings; observes with what regularity and precision they perform all their accustomed movements; ever moving, yet never conflicting; revolving side by side with their sister planets in love and harmony; subject to innumerable perturbations, yet never rebelling or spreading discord,—what an idea must such an one have of the greatness, love, power, and wisdom of that Being who made all these things, and how fitted to sympathize with the Psalmist in his outgushings, "Great and marvelous are thy works, Lord God Almighty; in wisdom hast thou made them all?"

When he goes forth into the vast field of nature, and attempts to explore her mysteries; observes the great law of gravitation, like the law of love in religion, ever drawing and binding the parts together; examines the means for the production and reproduction of plants; beholds their growth, decay, and reappearance in other and varied forms; is delighted with the gorgeous colors of the painted flower; sees the rich abundance that God has every-where thrown around us, as well as the wise and beneficent laws for the expanding and controlling of the powers of created objects,—in all these things does he truly read of God.

In the bowels of the rock-ribbed earth, he reads upon the stones the teachings of Deity. He sees the vast population that inhabited the earth years before man ever set foot upon the soil. He learns lessons of power, of providence, of wisdom, recorded, as with pen of iron, upon the flinty rock. He finds the stones of the field in league with the Bible, both teaching the same fact,——God, the Creator of the heavens and the earth.

When he examines the mechanism of his own system; the materials of its composition, and the part each organ is designed to perform; the fine adaptation of means to ends which every-where manifests itself; the wise and wonderful laws by which the limbs perform their functions, and the nerves act their part; how the heart accomplishes its vast work of purification, collecting and distributing, as from one huge reservoir, the life-giving current through the whole system; the wonderful construction of the brain, and its office as the organ of the mind; the mysterious process of growth and decay which is continually going on; the various ends to which this complicated machine may be applied,— when he examines all these relations, may he not, will he not exclaim with the Psalmist, "I am fearfully and wonderfully made?"

If he opens the page of history, reads the records of the past, and examines God's dealings with other nations, he will see all things under the control of some superintending Power who is overruling and guiding the same. He will see nation after nation rebelling against God, going farther and farther away from his counsels, condemned to be destroyed by others, and these in their turn destined, for a similar reason, to meet the same fate. He will see other peoples who trust in God and obey his precepts, gifted with the light of truth while all around is immersed in a worse than Egyptian darkness. As long as they heeded the teaching of a Divine Ruler, they were preserved from the power of internal faction and external foes, which had destroyed other nations. They grew up in wisdom and piety. Their rulers were men of integrity and uprightness. He will see wicked kings who were guilty of leading the people into idolatry, stricken from their thrones, and their mighty empires, which had terrified nations and astonished the world by their grandeur and magnificence, crushed to earth. Amid the din of battle, the rise and fall of empires, the crushing of kings, and the upbuilding of king-doms, he sees the church preserved, and the gospel of the Redeemer still safe. If not in the temple of the crowned monarch, it is found in the dwelling of the humble servant of Jehovah. If he thus carefully studies the history of by-gone ages, will he not more fully understand the truth that "happy is that people whose God is the Lord?"

Will not a man instructed in all these various departments of thought, have grander conceptions of God, of man, of time and eternity, of heaven and hell, of life and death, of all those main pillars in the temple of Christianity, than he who has scarcely been beyond the limits of English Grammar? Will not the mind of a Thomas Dick, Chalmers, Robert Hall, Luther, Melancthon, or Jonathan Edwards have nobler views of God, more enlarged ideas of Christianity, of God's infinity and goodness, than the man who has read the word of God, deprived of all these helps? With their minds burdened with such views of the Deity, with all their powers strung to the highest tension, thoroughly alive to the greatness and grandeur of the subjects with which they have to deal, the interests of time and eternity, of God and man pressing home upon their hearts, would they not be better fitted for the great work of teaching the people, than deprived of such training?

Aptness to teach implies qualifications, and these demand extensive scientific attainments; at least more than an ordinary acquaintance with the vast domain of science. In keeping with this view, I quote the pertinent remarks of the late Dr. Alexander of Princeton: "Indeed, to speak the truth, there is scarcely any science or branch of knowledge which may not be made subservient to theology. Natural history, chemistry, and geology have sometimes been of important service in assisting the biblical student to solve difficulties contained in Scripture; or in enabling him to repel the assaults of adversaries which were made under cover of these sciences. A general acquaintance with the whole circle of science is of more consequence to the theologian than at first sight appears. Not to mention the intimate connection which exists between all parts of truth, in consequence of which important light may be collected from the remotest quarters, it may be observed that the state of learning in the world requires the advocates of the Bible to attend to many things which may not in themselves be absolutely necessary. He must be able to maintain his standing as a man of learning. He must be able to converse on the various topics of learning with other literary men, otherwise due respect will not be paid to him, and his sacred office may suffer contempt, in consequence of his appearing to be ignorant of what it is expected all learned men should be acquainted with. "

He must defend the truth. Every minister, like Paul, " is set for the defense of the gospel." He must be able not only "to exhort, but convince the gainsayers." The armies of infidelity have planted their batteries, and are ready and waiting to hurl their leveled artillery at the fortress of Christianity, and woe be to that officer who is found wanting. Their sentinels are on the alert, and every avenue must be carefully guarded. We have nothing to fear unless we underrate the enemy, and allow ourselves to become the victims of a careless indifference. When wide awake to the contest, and knowing the strength of the enemy, the church has always sent forth her champions who have struck terror to the hearts of her foes, demolished their strongholds, and brought lasting honor to the cause of truth. We still find some who love darkness rather than light; whose whole aim is to weaken the strength of the Christian; throw doubt on the evidences of his faith; cut the cords that bind him to his God; banish true piety from the land, and make of this moral world a "waste, howling wilderness." The church has challenged her enemies to the contest, and her leaders, trust-

ing in the sword of the Lord and of Gideon, have done battle
for the truth, and have conquered. From the days of Por-
phyry and Celsus unto the present, she has been able to
withstand all opposition. Science, falsely so called, has been
arrayed against her, but true science has faithfully repelled
the dart. In the early history of the church, when infidelity
and error were running rampant ; when Arianism, Socinian-
ism, Sabellianism, Nestorianism, and a thousand other errors
had flooded the church, there were still some champions, who,
as one mighty breastwork, planted themselves on the defensive, and rolled back the fearful tide of sin. On through
every century, when there was danger, there were defenders.

A Watson is always found to fling back into his teeth the
ribaldry of a Tom Paine, or the falsehoods of a Voltaire.
The sophisms of Hume have met more than their match in
the logic of a Campbell. When the court was thronged with
literary infidels ; when the minds of the learned were verging
toward irreligion ; when moral gloom appeared to have
settled upon the land, then Bishop Butler arose, and with a
logic unsurpassed since the days of the apostles, with the
very weapons of his opponents, hurled blows upon them from
which they have not yet recovered. Cudworth, Boyle, Stil-
lingfleet, Newton, Leslie, Clark, Leland, Warburton, Watson,
Chalmers, Robert Hall, Edwards, Paley, with a host of others
of later date, McCosh, Rodgers, Buchanan, Hengstenberg,
Walker, Alexander, Hodge, Kirwan, and others of kindred
reputation, are names of which the church may justly feel
proud ; names that the world will not willingly let die ;
names that are interwoven with the existence of the Christian
church.

Infidelity still reigns, and champions for the truth are
wanted. Foes are at work without, attempting to destroy our
holy Christianity. They have changed their tactics, but are
as treacherous and warlike as ever. Having left the vantage

ground which metaphysics seemed to give them, they have planted themselves on the domain of science, to be in their turn dislodged from these fortifications, and driven from every covert. Physiology in infidel hands, is employed to disprove the unity of man. Geology is asked to tell a tale that shall contradict the Mosaic account of creation. Astronomy is bribed to testify that there has been no creation, but that the stars, with all the retinue of heaven, are but emanations from the great I AM. The records of Egypt and the sculptured tablets of Nineveh have been arrayed in battle against the chronology of Scripture. Natural science has been made to contradict the truth of a creation from nothing, and has accounted for all things by the theory of spontaneous generation, effects being produced by bodies coming in contact, subject to certain conditions and restrictions. A personal God has been denied, and the beauty and grandeur everywhere around us, manifesting to the Christian some bountiful Benefactor, are but part and parcel of the universal God, the *To Pan* of the Greeks. A Providence has been cast aside, and all things reduced to the control of natural laws, which are guided and controlled by nothing, and that these work out our happiness and misery. German rationalism, rather *ir*-rationalism, is busy, and would reduce every thing to mere reason; would strip the Bible of its divinity, and give us no more, if indeed as much, than the bald skeleton of truth. Every-where we see the opponents of the truth planting themselves for another attack. From the citadel of natural science they hope to cast their engines of destruction. Skillful in maneuvering, they must be met by men qualified to dislodge them from their position. You, and I, and others must see to it that the cause of our Master receives no injury. How shall we accomplish this herculean task unless prepared to give battle with their own weapons? To do this successfully, the weapons they brandish must be made the subject of special study.

The vigorous words of the lamented Hugh Miller are pertinent to this subject. Speaking of the study of the sciences, he says: "Judging from the preparations made in their colleges and halls, men do not now seem sufficiently aware —though the low thunder of every railway, and the snort of every steam engine, and the whistle of the wind amid the wires of every electric telegraph seem to publish the fact— that it is in the department of physics, not metaphysics, that the greater minds of the age are engaged; that the Lockes, Humes, Kants, Berkeleys, Dugald Stewarts, and Thomas Browns belong to the past; and that the philosophers of the present time, tall enough to be seen all the world over, are the Humboldts, the Aragos, the Agassizes, the Liebigs, the Owens, the Herschels, the Bucklands, and the Brewsters. The Cuviers, the Huttons, the Cavendishes, and the Watts, with their successors, the practical philosophers of the present age, men whose achievements in physical science we find marked on the surface of the country in characters which might be read from the moon, are not adequately represented (in our colleges). It would, perhaps, be more correct to say that they are not represented at all, and the clergy as a class suffer themselves to linger far in the rear of an intelligent laity, a full age behind the requirements of the time. Let them not shut their eyes to the danger which is obviously coming. The battle of the evidences will have as certainly to be fought on the field of *physical science*, as it was contested in the last age on that of metaphysics."

This brood of infidels is prolific. The men of Athens were accustomed to banish from their city the solitary skeptic who appeared among them. We have thrown down the gauntlet and challenged them to the contest, and it behooves us to prepare well for the struggle. We still have a Kant, a Compte with whom we must contend. Lamarck, Spinoza, Hegel, Strauss, and Schelling must be met. Carlyle yet writes. The sugar-coated skepticism of Holmes is doing its work upon the literary minds of the age. "Vestiges," "Cosmos," and the "Constitution of Man" are read and believed by many. Owen and his school are re-hashed to us in a new form almost every year. Mackey tells us of the "Progress of Intellect," and Professor Newman gives us his "Phases of Faith." Emerson and Parker speak to us of the "Infinite," the "Over-soul." D'Holbach treats us to cold materialism, while Harriet Martineau administers lessons on duty.

Our land is flooded with infidelity and infidel publications. The church must meet them and crush them. Hitherto she has proved herself to be more than a match for all her opponents. Shall she still retain that superiority, and show that she is equal to the contest, or sluggishly sit down while the enemy sows tares within her borders? The answer rests with you and with me. To whom shall the church, in her extremity, look for leaders if not to her ministers; and woe be to the church when she sends forth ignorant and untutored men to give battle to the powers of scientific infidelity. A Ball's Bluff or Manassas shall be the fate of the church when to unskillful hands she commits her destiny in the hour of trial. Difficulties in science and philosophy must be met. Scripture must be reconciled with science; passages of holy writ, with each other. By sound argument the church must meet and vanquish all opposition; must make the Bible, and reason, and revelation teach the same doctrine; must build around her possessions fortifications that the weapons of skepticism shall not be able to harm.

What saith the Scriptures? After all, these must be our guide. I have already referred to the example of the apostles, as affording no argument in favor of an ignorant ministry. I have shown that in the Jewish dispensation learned men were set apart for the service of the sanctuary. When God communed with men, he did so through intelligent mediums. He did not change that policy when the Christian dispensation was inaugurated. Almost the last message communicated by the great Apostle to Timothy was, "the things which thou hast heard of me among many witnesses, the same commit thou to faithful men who shall be able to instruct others also." How shall they teach unless qualified, and how qualify themselves unless by diligent, patient study? The same apostle writing to Titus, a youthful minister, exhorted him "to hold fast the faithful word as he had been taught"— by Paul himself, and not by inspiration—that he "may be able by sound doctrine both to exhort and convince the gainsayers." How shall he do this without a knowledge of the objections of his opponents, and the best method of refuting them? He also gives a reason for this : " For there are many unruly, and vain talkers, and deceivers, specially they of the circumcision, whose mouths must be stopped ; who subvert whole houses, teaching things which they ought not." It is the business of the minister to stop their mouths; and how shall he accomplish this work if his talk be as vain as their own. " But speak thou the things which become sound doctrine." How can he do this unless he first ascertain what sound doctrine demands? "Not giving heed to Jewish fables and commandments of men that turn from the truth." He must know what these are, so as to warn his flock against their evil tendency. " In doctrine showing uncorruptness, gravity, sincerity, soundness of speech, that can not be condemned." Can an ignorant man exhibit the soundness that the apostle demands? " Let no man despise thee." So preach and conduct yourself that no injury shall result to the cause of your Master from your teaching or your conduct. Paul informs Timothy of some who "desired to be teachers of the law, understanding neither what they say, nor whereof they affirm," and exhorts him to teach the law in all its purity, and not as others have done. He makes known to him the requisite qualifications. That he should not be a novice, but instructed in his work. Prophecies had been foretold to the intent that in the last days many should depart from the faith, and should teach false doctrines. He is authorized to put his brethren in remembrance of these things, and for so doing would be commended. But how teach his members, if he understood them not himself. In order to do this, he is commanded, "Till I come give attention to reading, to exhortation, to doctrine; neglect not the gift that is in thee; meditate on these things; give thyself wholly to them, that thy profit may appear unto all; take heed unto thyself and thy doctrine; continue in them, for in doing thus thou shalt save thyself and them that hear thee." If we must but open our mouths and the Spirit will fill them, as some wiseacres attempt to teach, why was Paul guilty of the consummate blunder of recommending reading and meditation to the youthful Timothy? "Keep that which is committed to thy trust, avoiding profane and vain babblings and oppositions of science, falsely so called." The way to do this was first to ascertain the nature of those scientific contradictions, if there were any. "Hold fast to the form of sound words which thou has heard of me." "Study to show thyself approved unto God, a workman that needeth not to be ashamed, rightly dividing the word of truth." Study the word and works of Deity. Qualify yourself for the arduous duties awaiting you, so that the church shall not be ashamed of your ministrations; and do all this that you may rightly divide and enforce the word of truth. Could stronger language be employed? "All Scripture is given by inspiration of God, and is profitable for doctrine, for reproof, for correction, for instruction in righteousness, that the man of God may be *thoroughly* furnished unto all good works." The minister, therefore, must be mighty in the Scriptures before he is properly fitted for his business. "When thou comest, bring with thee the books, and especially the parchments." Paul, with all his knowledge, found it necessary to consult books, and may even have had his written sermons. "I am set for the defense of the gospel." How defend it when you have no knowledge of the enemy, and are not qualified to repel his assaults? "Contend earnestly for the faith once delivered to the saints." Shall we not accomplish more if we go forth with a quiver full of arrows, than if we attempt to cope single handed? Paul boasted that he had not "shunned to declare unto them the whole counsel of God." Can a man do this when he is almost totally ignorant of a part of that counsel? "And he gave pastors and teachers, for the perfecting of the saints, for the work of the ministry, for edifying the body of Christ." How can a minister instruct and edify his people unless his knowledge be superior to theirs; and how can this be, in this enlightened age of the world, unless he be an intelligent man? "Every scribe which is instructed unto the kingdom of heaven is like unto a man that is an householder, who bringeth forth out of his treasures things new and old." But how can he do this if there be nothing in his treasury save the old, and that in homeopathic doses? We are told that "Ezra caused the people to understand the reading." So must the minister; and how can he unless he first understand it himself? The Scriptures every-where approve, yea, demand an intelligent ministry. The greatest wonder is, how any man who had carefully read them, should conclude that God chose ignorant and illiterate men as the embassadors of his kingdom.

The *Fathers* understood Christ as demanding an educated ministry, and for this purpose seminaries were established for the instruction of students in theology. At a very early period there was a seminary of high reputation in the city of Alexandria, in which candidates for the ministry were trained up together under the ablest instructors ; seminaries in which such men as Pantaenus, Clemens Alexandrinus, and Origen taught with eminent success. Eusebius and Jerome tell us that this seminary had existed and enjoyed a succession of able ministers from the time of Mark the Evangelist. Polycarp, a disciple of John the Apostle, we are told in ecclesiastical history, established a seminary at Smyrna. John himself founded one at Ephesus. Writers on Christian Antiquities teach us that at a very early period seminaries of a similar kind were found at Rome, Cesarea, Antioch, and other places, all of which accomplished a good work, and were thought essential to the honor and prosperity of the church.

Of course this action in the direction of learning met with some opposition. Says the historian Mosheim, "It must not be supposed that the Christian church was full of literary, wise, and scientific men. For there was no law as yet to prevent the ignorant and illiterate from entering the sacred office, and it appears from explicit testimony that many of both the bishops and presbyters were entirely destitute of science and learning. Besides, the party was both numerous and powerful, who considered learning as injurious, and even destructive to true piety." The existence of such schools shows how the leading minds of the age felt the necessity of an able ministry. Had such a ministry continued, the church would never have sunk to the depths of wretchedness which she experienced during the darkness of the middle ages.

Even at that early day, immediately after the establishment of Christianity, the presence of the Holy Spirit did not supersede the necessity of extensive knowledge, and thorough training in the embassador for Christ. Nor does he do so now. " The gods help those who help themselves."

What does history teach us of the mutual relation existing between learning and Christianity? The corruptions of Christianity, by which the simple apostolic ministry became a mediatory priesthood; and this priesthood built up into a mighty hierarchy; repentance was perverted into penance, and God's free gift of pardon was changed into the absolution of the priest, sold for money; the simple and touching sacrifice of Christ into idolatrous mummeries; the whole system of corruption which finally culminated in the Catholic Church,—all these were not the result of learning, but of ignorance. They grew out of the enthusiasm of perhaps honest, yet ignorant and misguided men. They grew to maturity, and culminated in an age when an unreading laity was led and instructed by an ignorant priesthood, who could not write their own sermons. With such a ministry, no wonder that a night of darkness settled upon the church. Like priest, like people. Christianity was lost sight of amid the darkness of a superstitious and ignorant age. But as soon as universities were founded, marts of intellectual commerce sprang up; metropolitan centers of discussion and inquiry were established. Then any man could have seen that a giant was born; an influence about to be exerted which would one day shake that mighty fabric, and scatter its foolish dogmas to the four winds. The Schoolmen came upon the stage. In these medieval schools, there was hewn and shaped together, with curious cutting and carving, that system of scholastic theology, of which much of the controversy of our day is but a reproduction. They did not elicit much new truth that was valuable, but they sharpened their powers for the work before them. Thought was stimulated, and a yearning for unknown truth created, which might serve to introduce the era of intellectual light that soon came.

As God from time to time raised up mighty champions, who shot like bolts of livid lightning across the vast expanse of mental gloom, who were they; what were they; and where were they found? Who, in the fourteenth century, aroused all England with his manly eloquence and vindicated

Scripture, in tones heard all over Europe? It was WICKLIFFE, trained in Oxford College, and crowned with academic honors. In that University of Oxford, he found a fit position and fit enginery for his attack upon the strongholds of superstition. In the next century who were the witnesses for Christ, before whom pontiff and emperor trembled, and the Council of Constance condemned to the flames? Go into their cells. Stand by the fires built for them in the meadow by the river-side. Listen to their testimony in prison and in flame. See their ashes mingled with the running waters! Who are they? Where were they trained? They are scholars—learned men. In the University of Prague they lifted up their voices for Christ, and from that university JOHN HUSS, and his companion JEROME, came to seal their testimony with their lives. Another century introduced the Reformation. Who accomplished that? "DOCTOR MARTIN LUTHER," as the Germans call him, was a finished scholar. His name is inseparable from the University of Wittenberg. The first gun fired in that struggle, was the nailing of Luther's theses for discussion, according to the scholastic forms of debate. The reformers were the learned men of their day. The age of the Reformation was the revival of learning. Look at history, and you will be compelled to confess that learning produced the Reformation. Why deny its power for good now?

Says Professor Tyler, in his excellent little work on "Prayer for Colleges," "The reformers—those before the Reformation, as well as the reformers usually so-called—Wickliffe, and Huss, and Reuchlin, and Erasmus, Luther, and Melancthon, and Bucer, and Calvin, and Tyndale, and Bilney, and Latimer, and Knox were men trained in the universities, and thus prepared by the providence, as well as the grace of God, for the work which they were destined to accomplish. It was while they were students in the university that new light dawned upon their souls, and the *Greek Testament*, accompanied in several instances by the Latin translation of Erasmus, was, to most of them, the source from whence the new light shone. The larger part of them were afterward professors in the universities, and from these fortresses of learning and influence they hurled their missiles at the corruptions of the papal church; from these centers of illumination they scattered light over the dark nations. *The Universities of Prague and Wittenbery, of Basle, and Lausanne, of Oxford and Cambridge, of Strasbury and St. Andrews, were the birth-places of the Reformation.*"

Next came the conflict of Puritanism with hierarchy. Whence came Puritanism? Where armed for the struggle? By the Cam and the Isis it gathered strength to battle with the storm. These universities of learning yielded their fruit, which still remains for the healing of nations. Next came the great Methodist awakening which stirred the English people, and is still telling happily upon the destiny of the world. Where was Methodism born? In an Oxford College, where a little company of scholars who believed that religion did not consist in dry formalities, but in the soul's experience, were wont to meet. Wesley and Whitefield were there. There was found the power that was to shake Great Britain, and spread beyond the ocean.

Samuel J. Mills, imbued with a zeal for God's cause, and burning with a desire for the conversion of the heathen world, collecting a few of his companions, went out into a field near to Williams College to pray for those who sit in darkness. Ere they left the "haystack," around whose base they had assembled, they pledged themselves not to rest until some movement should be set on foot, that would carry the gospel beyond the sea. This college student, with his associates, gave birth to the great AMERICAN MISSIONARY movement. The flame they kindled has been kept alive upon that and other altars. American missionaries have not only been

3*

learned men, but with few exceptions, have consecrated themselves to the noble work while engaged in college studies.

Time will not allow me to accumulate references. History is full of them. They all show that when a great work is to be performed, when a mighty impetus is to be communicated to the sluggish movements of the church, a learned man is called into the field to accomplish the mission. The founder of the church with which most of us stand connected—I mean William Otterbein—was a finished scholar, read in Latin, Greek, Hebrew, and Divinity. Could I write the influence of learning and learned men in furthering the interests of Christianity, and the untold good they have accomplished, I would simply write the history of the Christian church. On the other hand, when learning and religion have been separated, and made to travel their pathways alone ; when religion has discarded the abundance of aid which science has been willing to grant, the clergy are illiterate and blind, the laity go astray, and error and superstition like a dark pall, settle down upon the church. Let us read history to profit.

This age emphatically demands an educated ministry. In some respects it has no parallel. See the subtile infidelity which is every-where prevalent; approaching us very often in the guise of truth ; containing, as did the Indian's story, two truths to one lie; truth so skillfully interwoven with falsehood as to deceive the very elect; infusing itself into every system and every creed ; plying every means in its power for the accomplishment of its nefarious designs. How is the man of God to meet this? How recognize and refute it when he does meet it? Never before has such subtilty been manifested, and never before have skillful men been in so great demand. Now is the time spoken of by the prophet—now is his prediction verified: "The time will come when they will not endure sound doctrine, but after their own lusts they will heap to themselves teachers having itching ears. And they shall turn away their ears from the truth, and shall be turned unto fables."

This age is independent in thought—is inquisitive. Mankind now, more than ever, refuse to be satisfied with an *ipse dixit*. Men have been priest-led That time has passed, and the strings are broken. Now they want information, but desire to form their own conclusions. The thunders of the Inquisition no longer compel them to think as the church thinks. This spirit pervades all the departments of life, of literature, of morals. Fulsome bombast, high-sounding phrases, vehement declamation, huge *"sesquipedalia verba"* will no longer avail. By the serious, religion is thought too important a matter to be trifled with; by the trifling, empty declamation is turned into foolishness. But one way to meet this spirit,—qualify your teachers.

This is a thinking age. Never was man so wakeful as now. He is not content to remain where his father was, but is ever seeking new truths; prying into new difficulties. He is not satisfied with the surface, but must probe deeper. He is fiercely iconoclastic. Nothing too holy, nothing too sacred to escape his scrutiny. Books and papers are every-where prevalent. All men read, and he who reads thinks. "Beware," says an able New England writer, "when God lets loose a thinker upon this planet. Then all things are at work. There is not a principle in science but its flank may be turned to-morrow. There is not any literary reputation, not the so-called eternal names of fame, that may not be revised and condemned. The very hopes of man, the thoughts of his heart, the religion of nations, the manners and morals of mankind are all at the mercy of a new generalization." Never before were so many thinkers let loose.

All these matters must be considered by the man who aspires to be a teacher in sacred things. To properly fill this position, the brightest qualifications are not too bright; the most brilliant talents none too brilliant; the most profound scholarship none too profound; the most varied powers none too quick or various. Such a man is properly qualified " to rightly divide the word of truth. "

Time passes, and I must be brief. The subject is inexhaustible. In its contemplation, thoughts crowd thick and fast upon the mind. I can not now speak of the great need of a scientific education to the missionary, who is not only required to preach the gospel, but often the civil and ecclesiastical interests of the people rest in his hands, and he must devote a portion of his time to these if he would establish a permanent church. He must be able to teach science as well as religion, because the religious systems of the heathen are built upon a scientific foundation, and if you destroy these pillars, the edifice must fall. " Thus the Hindoo religion can not stand without Hindoo astronomy and cosmogony. Science undermines the pillars of heathenism, and frightens its votaries from its tottering walls. " I can barely refer to the fact that most of our colleges have been established by ministers; that the larger portion of the professors are drawn rom the ranks of the clergy; that they to a great extent form and control the educational sentiment of a people, and hereby hold in their hands a mighty power for the accomplishment of good, which it were worse than madness to cast aside; that the people of this age are a reading people, and demand the proper class of books and periodicals; that new books of theology are to be written; newspapers are to be edited; tracts to be prepared for distribution among the people; quarterly reviews to be conducted; that facts in science and history are being made known, and must be applied to the elucidation of Scripture texts; that different passages must be examined in the light of present scientific attainments. Some must undertake the work, and who so likely to be called to the task as the students of our colleges? That the work of the minister is a laborious one, affording little time for study, and that his preparation must be made before he enters upon the cares and duties of a pastor's life; that ignorance usually weakens the minister's power for good, and is the source of incalculable evils, productive of all forms of error, as the history of the church will abundantly testify; that a pastor's influence, as a general rule, other things being equal, has always been in proportion to his learning,—all these would afford interesting topics for discussion.

I have omitted to answer several objections which are often urged against this position. I have done so because they did not seem to me very important. If the view I have presented be correct, there can be no insurmountable objections.

It may appear to some of you that I have erected a high standard. No higher than the Bible and reason demand. Both alike ask that the minister of God be *thoroughly* furnished. While contending for such quailifications in the men who now enter the ministry, I do not mean to say that a man can do no good and should not preach unless he is a finished scholar. The church is full of men, who deprived of all the advantages which we enjoy, with but the rudiments of learning, yet having a heart burning with a zeal for their fellow-men, have counted nothing dear to them that they might win souls to Christ. There may be before me to-night men who have nobly battled for the truth; men, "the latchets of whose shoes I am unworthy to unloose;" men, who amid toils, and dangers, and afflictions, have lived for Christ, and labored to bring their erring brethren back to the bosom of their father, God. Their labors have been blessed, and many are the stars that shall shine in their crowns of rejoicing. Far be it from me to detract one iota from the honor which they have richly deserved. For well do I know the mighty work they have accomplished, and the labors they have put forth for the welfare of the church. Like the widow, they have given every thing, and that God who sees all things, will reward them for their actions. But to you, young gentlemen, living in this age of the world when so much is demanded of the ministry, if you neglect the means of improvement now afforded ; if you weaken the influence you could and should possess, and thereby injure the cause of your Master, and be instrumental in the destruction of your fellow-men, you will be deserving of blame, and the great God will not hold you guiltless. Our fathers have almost finished their work. They will soon hear the message, "Come up higher." Upon you and upon me rests the welfare of Zion. The eternal destinies of mankind are in our hands. Shall we shoulder the responsibility, and quit us like men? or shall we become foolish triflers in the great work? The character of the ministry, and the consequent standing of the next age, rest upon the young men who are now preparing to enter the sacred office. Away with the idea that God calls triflers into the church. That while a thorough qualification is necessary for the business pertaining to this life, the grossest ignorance will not exclude one from entering the office of the ministry ! *We want a higher standard ;* want no man commissioned to preach the gospel who is totally unfitted for the work. I urge upon you to magnify the office, and fit yourselves for properly discharging all its duties. "Study to show yourselves approved of God; workmen that need not to be ashamed, rightly dividing the word of truth."

Gentlemen, it may be that I address you for the last time. Indulge me a moment longer. I know not how many of you will go forth as embassadors for Christ. I know that thousands are wanted. "The harvest is indeed plenteous, but the laborers are few." From almost every land there is a call for the bread of life. India has opened wide her gates. Japan, long closed against them, now demands religious teachers. The sunny plains of AFRICA are ready for the white man. From every continent, from every island, from every nook and corner of the habitable earth comes the pleading cry, "Come over and help us." Do you hear the call? Will you heed it? Within the last few months our own "Barbary States" have been opened to men who are not afraid to preach a pure gospel. Never was there such a demand for an able ministry. Appreciate your position. Awake to the responsibilities resting upon you. Go forth to the contest "thoroughly furnished," and then "quit yourselves like men." Go forth with a double portion of the Spirit's influence resting upon you. And whether called to labor in your native land, or summoned to preach the gospel beyond the sea; whether you shall lead a quiet, peaceful life, or like the devoted missionary, be compelled to seal your testimony with your blood, I urge, I entreat, I implore you, in the words of the lamented Tyng, "STAND UP FOR JESUS." When you have finished your work, and have been summoned higher, may it be written of each of you,

"He fell like a Martyr; He died at his Post."